Colouring Book for Nationalist Children

Mathew D. Staunton

The Onslaught Press

This book is dedicated to all children
who have suffered in the name of abstract concepts
like nationalism and republicanism
at the hands of those who should have been protecting them

and also to Aoife

<3

Published in Oxford by The Onslaught Press
11 Ridley Road, OX4 2QJ
December, 2013

This edition, text, and illustrations © 2013 Mathew D. Staunton

All rights reserved. No part of this publication may be
reproduced, stored in a retrieval system, or transmitted,
in any form or by any means, electronic, mechanical,
photocopying, recording, or otherwise, without the prior
permission in writing of the publisher, or as expressly
permitted by law, or under terms agreed with the
appropriate reprographics rights organization

ISBN-13 978-0-9927238-1-1

Printed by LightningSource.

Note to Parents

This little book has been conceived and produced at the request of our wise leaders by the most patriotic artists in our beloved country. It is intended as an enjoyable pedagogical tool to help you in the satisfactory training of your children. The future of our great Nation depends upon our children and they must be made to understand their duties and the sacred cause of their forefathers.

Remember to explain the importance of each image and the corresponding concepts in the context of our terrible struggle for Independence, our many martyred heroes, and our glorious victory over the cowardly enemies who barred our way to civilization for so long.

All honour to the Nation.

OUR INDUSTRY

OUR LANGUAGE

OUR LAND

OUR FOOD

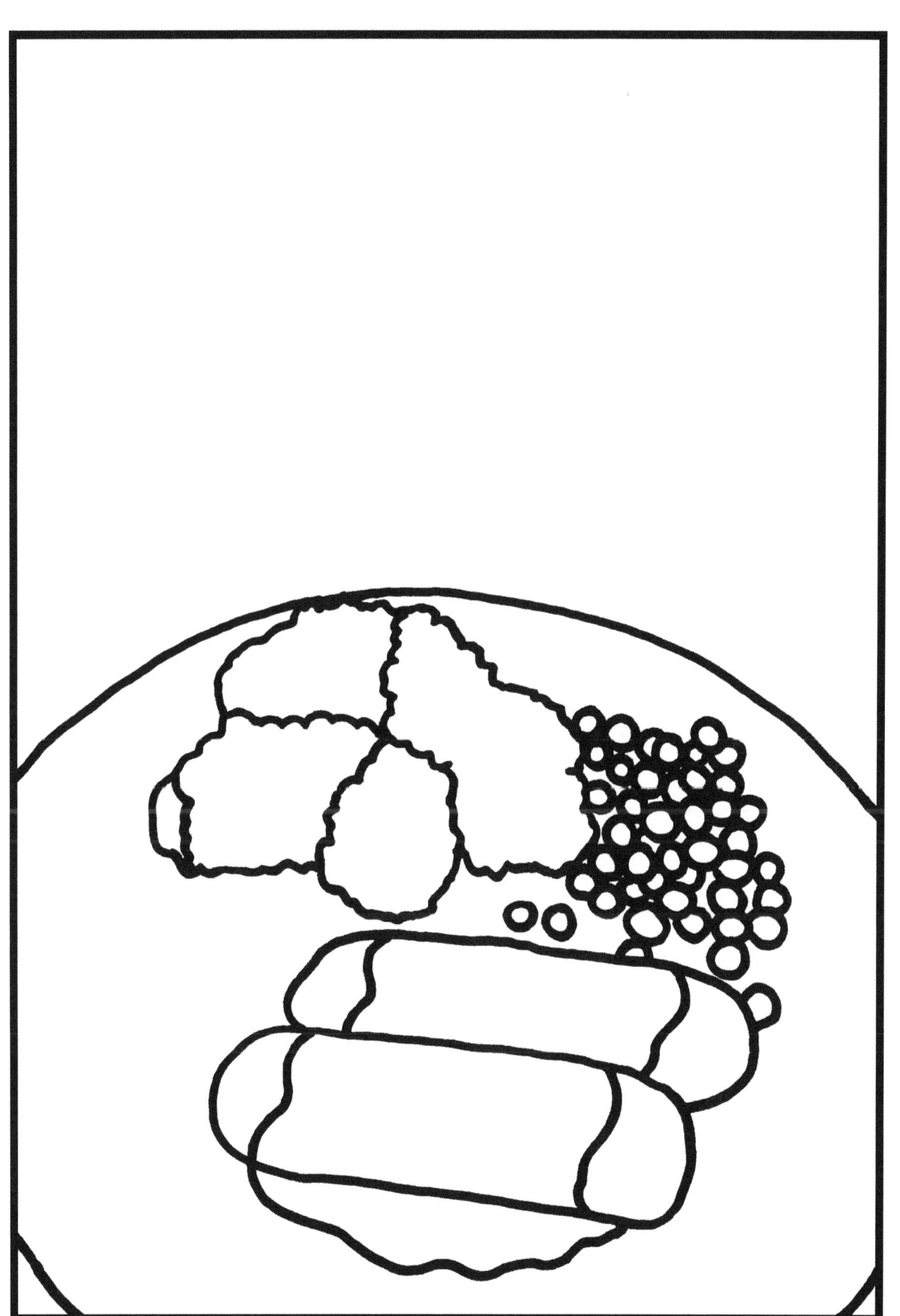

OUR ENEMIES

OUR GAME

OUR HERITAGE

OUR HEROES

OUR COSTUME

OUR NAVY

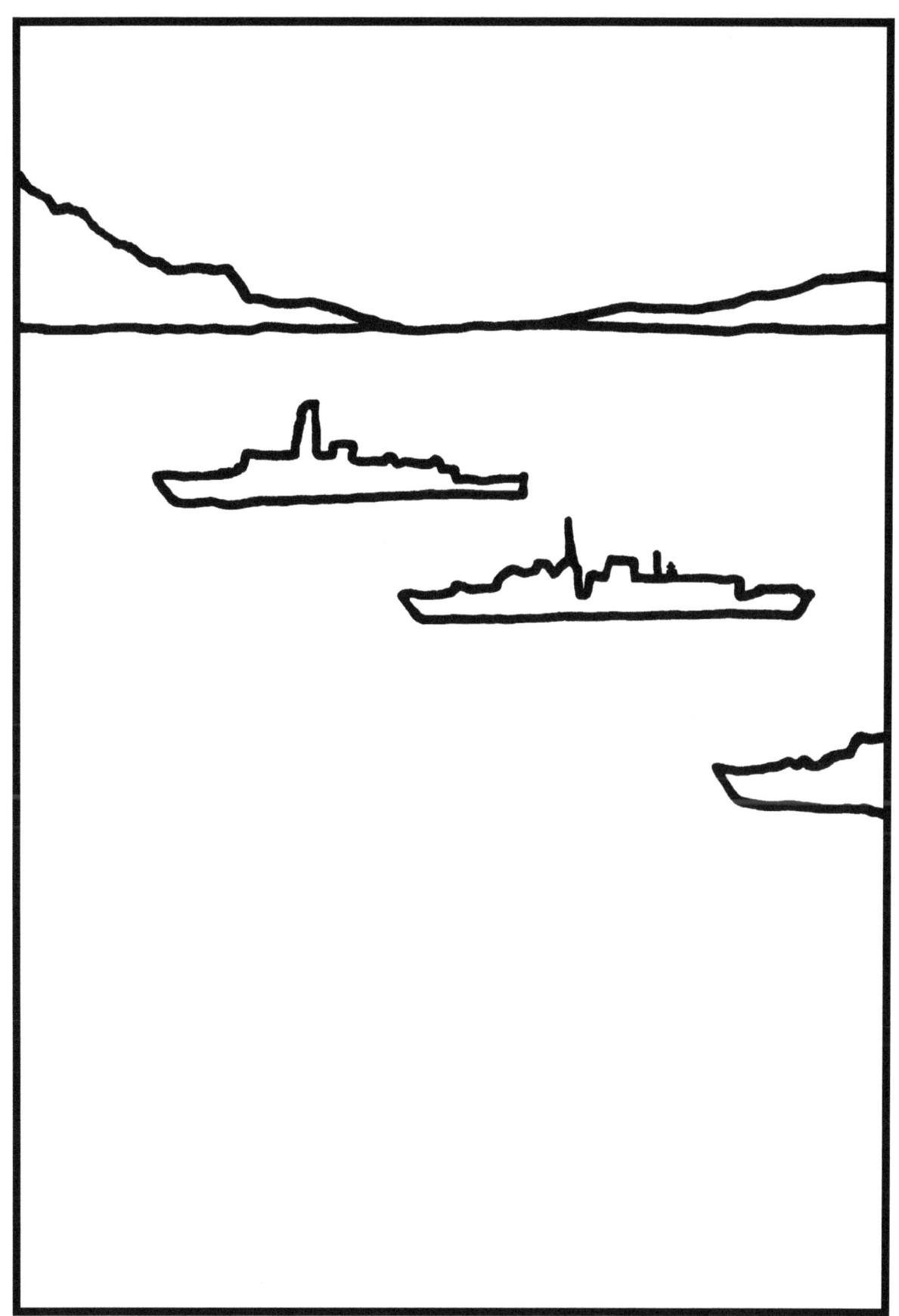

OUR BATTLEFIELD

OUR LEADERS

OUR CHILDREN

Lightning Source UK Ltd.
Milton Keynes UK
UKHW032225060121
376553UK00003B/16